THE UNITED KINGDOM

Written and photographed by
Christa Stadtler

Our Country

Australia
Canada
China
France
Greece
India
Italy
Japan
New Zealand
Pakistan
Spain
The United Kingdom
The United States
West Germany

Cover *A hillside village in West Yorkshire, northern England. The surrounding fields are broken up by typical stone walls.*

Editor: Anna Girling
Designer: David Armitage

First published in 1991 by
Wayland (Publishers) Ltd
61 Western Road, Hove
East Sussex BN3 1JD, England

© Copyright 1991 Wayland (Publishers) Ltd

British Library Cataloguing in Publication Data
Stadtler, Christa
  The United Kingdom.— (Our country)
  I. Title II. Series
  914.1

HARDBACK ISBN 1-85210-969-6

PAPERBACK ISBN 0-7502-0911-9

Typeset by Dorchester Typesetting Group Ltd
Printed in Italy by Rotolito Lombarda S.p.A.

All words printed in **bold** are explained in the glossary on page 30.

Contents

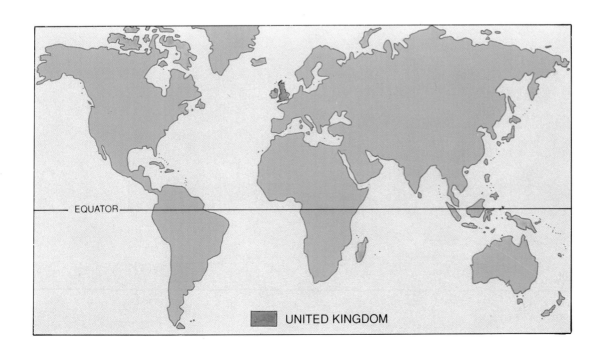

EQUATOR

UNITED KINGDOM

We live in the United Kingdom

This beautiful, wild moor in northern England is crossed by traditional old stone walls.

The United Kingdom is a group of islands on the western edge of Europe. England, Scotland and Wales are on one large island, called Great Britain. Northern Ireland is also part of the United Kingdom.

The main hills and mountains in Britain are in Scotland, Wales and northern and western England. There are rolling hills in central England and flatter plains in East Anglia and the south-east. Northern Ireland is hilly, with lakes and a rugged coastline.

England has the United Kingdom's biggest **population**. London is the **capital** city. The country is called the United Kingdom because it has a King or Queen, although it is governed by **Parliament**.

In this book, twelve children will tell you about life in the United Kingdom.

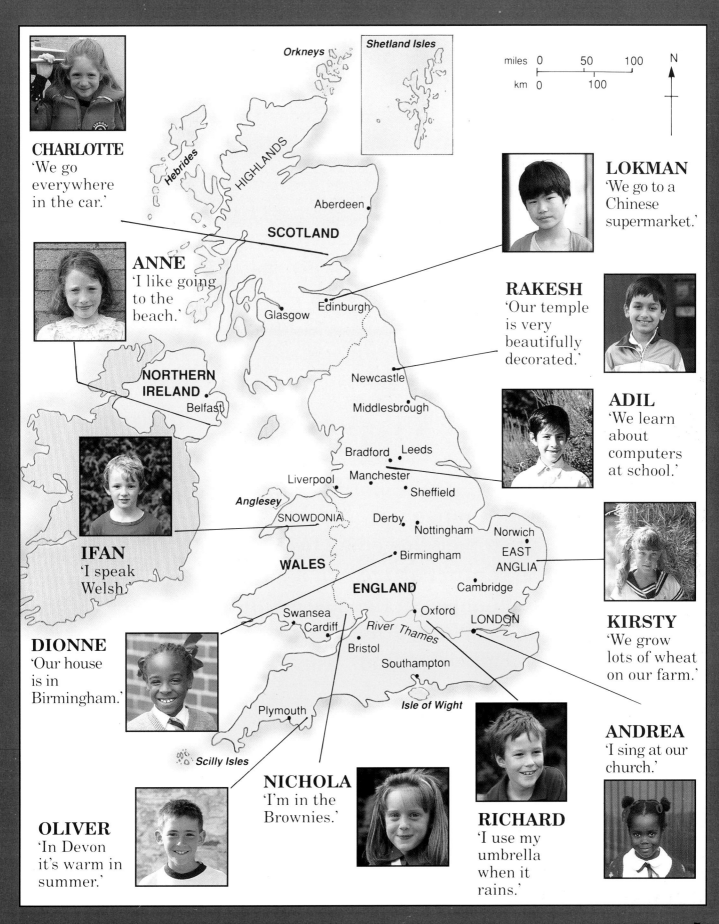

CHARLOTTE
'We go everywhere in the car.'

ANNE
'I like going to the beach.'

IFAN
'I speak Welsh.'

DIONNE
'Our house is in Birmingham.'

OLIVER
'In Devon it's warm in summer.'

NICHOLA
'I'm in the Brownies.'

LOKMAN
'We go to a Chinese supermarket.'

RAKESH
'Our temple is very beautifully decorated.'

ADIL
'We learn about computers at school.'

KIRSTY
'We grow lots of wheat on our farm.'

ANDREA
'I sing at our church.'

RICHARD
'I use my umbrella when it rains.'

Orkneys

Shetland Isles

miles 0   50   100
km 0   100

N

Hebrides

HIGHLANDS

Aberdeen

SCOTLAND

Glasgow   Edinburgh

NORTHERN
IRELAND
Belfast

Newcastle

Middlesbrough

Bradford   Leeds
Liverpool   Manchester
Sheffield

Anglesey
SNOWDONIA   Derby
Nottingham   Norwich
EAST
ANGLIA
Birmingham
WALES   Cambridge
ENGLAND
Swansea   Oxford
Cardiff   River Thames   LONDON
Bristol
Southampton

Plymouth   Isle of Wight

Scilly Isles

The weather

Even in summer, organizers of outdoor events cannot be sure of a sunny day, but rain has not stopped people enjoying this carnival.

British weather can change very quickly, with beautiful sunshine followed by heavy rain showers. The **temperature** can also vary quickly, with changes in the season and direction of the wind. Winds from the west are usually warm and wet. Winds from the east are cold and dry.

Westerly winds, bringing cloud and rain, are common. Most rain falls over the mountains in the west, especially Snowdonia in Wales and the Scottish Highlands. This can turn to sleet and snow in winter. The south coast of England is the sunniest part of the country.

'In Devon palm trees grow in the gardens.'

'I am Oliver. I live near the seaside in Devon. In winter it is often rainy and stormy here, but in summer it is usually warm. The last two summers were very hot indeed. The temperature got to 30 °C and there was hardly any rain for three months. Here I am with my father in front of Torquay pavilion.'

'I have an umbrella for when it rains.'

'My name is Richard. I live in Henley-on-Thames in Oxfordshire. You can see in the picture that it has just rained. I've got my umbrella and I'm wearing my waterproof coat. I don't like it when it rains, but it often does!'

The Gulf Stream, a current of warm water in the Atlantic Ocean, warms the west coast of Britain and Northern Ireland. Northern Ireland and parts of western Scotland are warm enough for palm trees to grow!

Farming and fishing

In the hills of north-west England, Wales and Scotland, farmers keep cattle and sheep. Sheep can live through the cold winters on the hills and **moors.** Their wool is made into cloth which is famous throughout the world.

The south-west of England has rich grass for feeding dairy cows. They produce milk used to make delicious ice cream and cheese.

Grain, potatoes and sugar beet are grown in south-east England and the lowlands of Scotland. In East Anglia, wheat, barley and **rape** grow in enormous fields. Farmers use big tractors and **combine harvesters** to plant and cut their crops.

A few fishing boats still work from this small harbour in Northern Ireland.

'We keep sheep and a few cows on our farm in Wales.'

'I am Ifan. Here I am with some of our sixteen dairy cows. We also keep about three hundred sheep, but they are out on the hills at the moment. Dad milks the cows twice a day and my brother and I often watch. In spring we help to feed the calves.'

'We grow lots of wheat and barley.'

'I am Kirsty. My father runs our family farm in East Anglia. We grow lots of wheat and barley, some rape and beans. The wheat and barley are usually harvested in the middle of August. Dad uses a combine harvester to cut the corn. Here he is testing the wheat to see if it is ready for cutting.'

Fishing was once very important. Today, though, there are very few fishing boats. Most fish are caught off the coasts of Scotland and north-east England.

Industry and jobs

Britain was one of the first countries to have heavy industries. With its coal and iron mines, Britain had the **natural resources** to make **textiles**, steel and ships. Today, coal and textiles can be produced more cheaply in other countries, and many British factories and mines have closed.

Now, Britain makes computers, **chemicals** and cars instead. Japanese car makers have built factories in Britain and now employ many people.

In Belfast, in Northern Ireland, the main industry for many years was shipbuilding.

Luxury Lotus sports cars are built at this small factory in East Anglia.

'My father checks the machines at this factory.'

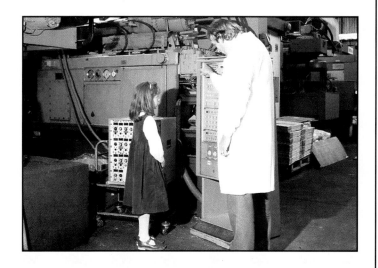

'I am Nichola. My father works at a factory that makes plastic bottles. The huge machines you can see in the picture make the bottles. There are lots of machines and only a few people to work them.'

'Mum looks after old people at a home.'

'I am Dionne. My mother works at a home for old people. The oldest woman is nearly one hundred years old. Sometimes Mum works late and I meet her at the home. Here we are celebrating Doris's ninetieth birthday.'

Now, few ships are built and many people have lost their jobs.

London is one of the world's most important centres for financial services such as banking and insurance. **Tourism** is an important industry and millions of people visit the United Kingdom every year.

Schools

School usually starts at nine o'clock in the morning and finishes at about three o'clock in the afternoon. There is a break of one hour at lunchtime. Some children eat a hot school meal but others bring sandwiches from home for lunch.

Most schools are free, but some parents pay for their children to go to private schools. Just to be confusing, some of these private schools are called 'public' schools!

English is the first language in school, except in parts of Wales where lessons are taught in Welsh.

Many children have to wear a uniform in the school's colours.

12

Children have to go to school from the age of five until they are sixteen years old. There are a few nursery schools for children under five.

'At my school everybody speaks and writes in Welsh.'

'I am Ifan. I go to a very small village school in Wales. There are only twenty-seven pupils in the whole school, which is quite nice. We have two classes, one for five to seven-year-olds and the other for seven to eleven-year-olds. Here I am writing in Welsh. "Yr haul" means "the sun".'

'I like using the computer at school.'

'I am Adil. At school we have English, maths and science lessons in the mornings. For science we are learning about weather, plants and computers. In the afternoons we have painting, singing and sport. Here my teacher is correcting my maths book.'

Religion

The main religion in the United Kingdom is **Christianity**. Most Christians belong to the Churches of England and Scotland. These are Protestant Churches. The Queen is head of the Church of England. There are also very many Roman Catholics.

In Northern Ireland about two-thirds of the people are Protestant and one-third Roman Catholic. Many people in Northern Ireland go to church regularly. In Britain, however, less than a quarter of people belong to a Christian religion.

There are many other religions. People

There are many pretty, old village churches dotted all over the countryside.

who came to live in the United Kingdom from other parts of the world brought their religions with them. There are now large groups of **Muslims**, **Hindus** and **Sikhs**. There are also many **Jewish** people in the United Kingdom.

'I like the music at our church.'

'I am Andrea. My family and I are Christians and we go to our Pentecostal church every Sunday. All the children spend half an hour studying the Bible. Singing is an important part of the service and we have a big band to lead the songs. Here I am playing with the band.'

'I go to the temple every Saturday.'

'I am Rakesh. My brother and I go to the Hindu temple every Saturday. We learn about Hinduism. We are also learning Hindi, a language spoken in India. Here you can see me inside the temple. It is beautifully decorated for a festival.'

Festivals

At Christmas most towns and cities put up special lights. These are in Oxford Street, London.

Most people celebrate the main Christian festivals of Christmas and Easter, even if they do not go to church. At Christmas, families decorate their houses with Christmas trees, give presents and get together for a big meal of roast turkey followed by Christmas pudding.

Scottish people like to celebrate New Year's Eve, which they call Hogmanay. On Bonfire Night (November 5) people build bonfires and set off fireworks to remember Guy Fawkes, who was caught trying to blow up the Houses of Parliament in 1605.

Muslims celebrate the end of Ramadan, the month of fasting, by praying to Allah (God), eating good food and giving presents. Hindus and Sikhs celebrate *Diwali*, a colourful festival of lights, in the autumn.

'My mother has made a huge meal for the festival.'

'I am Adil. Today we are celebrating a Muslim festival called *Eid al-Adha*. Lots of family and friends will visit us to give us their good wishes and eat with us. Here you can see my mother serving out the huge meal, which she spent all yesterday cooking.'

'The fair comes to Newcastle once a year.'

'I am Rakesh and I live in Newcastle upon Tyne. Every summer there is a fair. Here I am riding a horse on the merry-go-round. There are so many rides, like the ghost train, the big wheel and the helter-skelter, that it is hard to choose.'

In the summer there are many street festivals, village fairs and town carnivals all over the United Kingdom. In August in Notting Hill, London, there is a huge West Indian street carnival.

Homes

Most people live in or around large cities and towns. Cities like London, Glasgow and Manchester have grown and swallowed up villages and towns around them.

In the 1960s many high-rise blocks of flats were built, but most people prefer to live in houses. Many new estates of small houses with tiny gardens have been built. Most new housing has been built in the **suburbs** of towns and cities, so people spend a lot of time travelling from home to their jobs in the city centres.

Many British people love old houses. Buildings are carefully modernized so that they do not lose their pretty old windows, doors, beams and fireplaces.

Many British people prefer houses to flats. Each of these new houses in south London has a garden.

More than two-thirds of people own their homes. There is also **council housing** for people who cannot buy their own home and need somewhere to live.

'We have a climbing frame in our garden.'

'I am Dionne and I live in Birmingham. From our house it takes twenty minutes by bus to get to the city centre. Our house has three bedrooms and I share my bedroom with one of my sisters. All the houses in our area have large gardens. Here I am going shopping with my mother.'

'My grandparents' house is very old.'

'My name is Kirsty. This is my grandparents' house on our family farm. There is a date on the door which says 1645, but parts of the house were probably built before then. My grandmother thinks it was just a barn for animals to begin with. Everyone who works on the farm has lunch in the big kitchen.'

Sport and pastimes

Many children train with their local soccer club.

At school children learn sports such as soccer, hockey and netball in winter and athletics and cricket in summer.

Soccer is very popular all over the United Kingdom, both to watch and to play. In England cricket is played in the summer. In Wales many people like rugby football and in Scotland they play shinty, which is a kind of hockey.

Fishing, tennis and walking are very popular activities. A lot of young people are keen on skateboarding and windsurfing.

The British spend much of their spare time watching television. A large number of homes now have video recorders. Reading and going to the cinema are other pastimes.

'This is our favourite beach.'

'My name is Anne. Here I am with my sisters at our favourite beach. I am on the right. We like climbing around on the rocks, looking for pretty pebbles and shells. Sometimes we find crabs. You have to know how to hold them so that they don't pinch you. We usually get very wet paddling.'

'Brownies wear a special brown uniform.'

'My name is Nichola and I belong to the Brownies. There are Brownie groups all round the country. We play games, sing songs and go on nature walks. If we pass special tests we get badges to sew on our uniforms. To get a new badge I have got to play the piano for all the other Brownies. Here I am practising.'

Seaside towns, with fun-fairs, amusement arcades and stalls, are popular for holidays and day trips. Many people go abroad for their holidays.

Food

The traditional British breakfast of eggs, bacon, sausages and tomatoes is famous all over the world. Many people, however, prefer to start the day with cereal or toast with tea or coffee.

Lunch is usually a sandwich or quick snack. Most people eat their main meal, often a meat dish with vegetables, in the evening. Young children, though, probably eat a fairly big lunch and have a small supper in the evening.

On Sundays many families enjoy a traditional lunch of roast meat, roast

Fish and chips, from a fish and chip shop, are a traditional British takeaway meal. They are wrapped in paper to keep them warm.

potatoes and vegetables. Quite a lot of people, especially young people, prefer not to eat meat and have become **vegetarians**.

There are many regional dishes, such as Yorkshire pudding, Irish stew, Welsh rarebit (toasted cheese) and Scottish haggis (meat and oats boiled in a skin).

'Every day two children help to serve the school meal.'

'I am Adil. I eat at school every day. Today we are having spicy kebabs, chips and peas. Our school started serving **halal meat** about a year ago. Before then all the Muslim children only ate fish or eggs. Here I am serving the kebabs.'

'Lots of pubs sell food.'

'My name is Charlotte. Here I am with my mother and brother having lunch at the **pub**. Lots of pubs sell food. I'm not allowed inside the pub because I am too young, but I can sit outside. I am having bacon-and-egg flan. Mum is having a big salad.'

Shopping

This shopping street in Chester has been paved over so that shoppers are not troubled by traffic.

Most people shop once a week or once a month at a supermarket, where there is a large choice of goods. People drive to the enormous supermarkets which have been built on the edges of many towns. There are also small, local shops, where people buy fresh foods.

British people like to have their milk and newspapers delivered. First thing in the morning milk vans go from house to house leaving bottles of milk on the doorsteps.

In cities and big towns there are **department stores** selling household goods. Many towns now have shopping **precincts**, where cars are not allowed.

'The butcher calls at our house twice a week.'

'My name is Anne. My family lives in the countryside. Our baker and butcher have vans and they call at our house twice a week. The butcher sells vegetables, tinned food and sweets as well as meat. When he calls, my mother usually buys us all a treat. Even the dog gets a bone.'

'Many foods in this supermarket come from China.'

'My name is Lokman. In this picture my mother and I are shopping at a Chinese supermarket. My mother needs lots of special foods, like noodles, dried mushrooms and bean sprouts, for cooking our Chinese meals.'

Markets are held all over the country, with stalls selling everything from vegetables to clothes. In areas with big Asian and Chinese populations shops sell the special vegetables and spices used in their cooking.

Transport

Most people travel by car and most goods are transported by road. New motorways and roads are being built all the time, but traffic jams are still common.

The United Kingdom has an important railway network used by many travellers. Three million people use London's underground railway, called the 'tube', every day. Cities such as Manchester are trying to provide more bus and train services, but in country areas there is little **public transport**, so most people need a car.

Ferries cross to other parts of Europe, Northern Ireland and the Scottish islands. The Channel Tunnel, being built beneath the English Channel, will provide a rail link to France.

The M25, which circles London, is one of the country's newest and busiest motorways.

London Heathrow and London Gatwick are two of the world's busiest airports. There are flights to all parts of the world, as well as to Northern Ireland, Scotland and the United Kingdom's main cities.

'We go into London on the tube.'

'I am Andrea and I live in London. We use the car to drive to the shops and to my school, but when we want to go to the zoo or go shopping in the centre of London we travel on the tube. If we took the car we would probably get stuck in a traffic jam – and it takes ages to park.'

'My mother and father both have cars.'

'I am Charlotte. I live in the countryside in Scotland. My father has to drive all over Scotland and England for his job. There are no trains and buses near us and my mother takes us everywhere in the car. Here we are getting into my family's car after a trip on the river in a boat.'

Let's discuss the United Kingdom

Now that you have learned something about the United Kingdom, think about your own way of life. Is your school similar to Adil's or Ifan's? Does your mother have a job like Dionne's? Do your parents have cars like Charlotte's?

Ifan grows up speaking Welsh and English. Rakesh learns Hindi at the temple. Adil speaks Urdu, a language from Pakistan, at home. Are there people living near you who speak a different language, follow a different religion, or whose families come from another country?

Houses cluster around a village church.

Facts
Population: 57 million
Capital: London
Main language: English
Money: Pounds
Religion: Mainly Christian, also Muslim, Jewish, Hindu and Sikh

Many of Britain's historical sites have become tourist attractions. The Tower of London, an old fortress, is guarded by wardens called beefeaters.

When you go to the shops, or watch television, do you see things that were made in the United Kingdom? If you live in the United Kingdom, look for things from abroad and try to find out where they came from, and why.

Some of the most rugged and beautiful countryside in the United Kingdom can be found in Wales.

Glossary

Capital The most important city in a country.

Chemicals Products such as medicines, cosmetics and cleaning liquids.

Christianity A religion based on the teachings of Jesus Christ. There are many Christian groups. Roman Catholics are led by the Pope in Rome. Protestants split from the Catholic Church over 400 years ago.

Combine harvesters Huge machines for cutting crops and separating the grain from the stalks.

Council housing Houses and flats owned by the local government.

Department stores Big shops which sell many different goods.

Halal meat Meat prepared following Muslim laws.

Hindus People who follow the Hindu religion. They pray to many gods and goddesses.

Jewish Belonging to the Jewish religion, based on the Old Testament of the Bible.

Moors Large areas of land, covered with rough grass, found in northern and western England.

Muslims People who follow the Islamic religion. They pray to Allah (God) and follow the teachings of the Prophet Muhammad.

Natural resources Useful things found in or on the ground, such as coal, trees and water.

Parliament The group of people who rule the United Kingdom.

Population The number of people in a country.

Precinct An area of a town that is closed off.

Pub Short for 'public house'. A place where people can buy drinks and food and chat with friends.

Public transport The system of trains, buses and undergrounds in a country.

Rape A plant with bright yellow flowers and seeds which produce oil, used for cooking.

Sikhs People who follow the Sikh religion, based on the teachings of a holy man called Guru Nanak.

Suburbs Areas of houses on the edges of towns and cities.

Temperature A measurement of how hot or cold something is.

Textiles All kinds of cloth.

Tourism The industry dealing with holidays and travel.

Vegetarians People who choose not to eat meat.

Books to read

Britain is My Country, Bernice and
  Cliff Moon (Wayland, 1984)
*Great Britain – The Land and its
  People*, Anna Sproule
  (Macdonald, 1986)
*The National Trust Picture Atlas of
  Britain*, Avril Lethbridge
  (Kingfisher, 1987)
United Kingdom, Neil Grant
  (Macmillan, 1988)

Picture acknowledgements

All photographs are by Christa Stadtler except: Eye Ubiquitous 22, 24; Tony
Stone Worldwide 28; Simon Warner cover. Maps on contents page and
page 5 supplied by Jenny Hughes.

Index